ERGONOMICS OF THE ABSURD

by Alex Victor
The World's Greatest Ergonomist!!

Dedicated to:
Bruce W., Jim B., Gene A. Dieter J.
Real Mentors & Friends, Whom I Miss Terribly.
They Taught Me How to Laugh & Learn

About the Author

Alex Victor is a real life, award winning, vastly experienced, credentialed nationally prominent Professional Ergonomist, with an outstanding sense of humor albeit a bit nerdy.

He is expert in Ergonomic analysis, workstation design, equipment design & fabrication, productivity enhancements, tool design and workflow & methods analysis, and especially taking away injured worker's pain, much to their happiness.

You can usually find him in his shop, preferable to his office developing high level creative solutions to the most difficult occupational injury projects in Fortune 500 & Public Sector organizations.

Experienced in machining, mechanics, fabrication and prototyping, he designs, fabricates, tests, & installs custom solutions / tools / workstations for virtually any (difficult) occupation and/or workstation correction. Workers helped include musicians, industry workers, police officers, construction workers, heavy machine operators, cooks and of course computer users (plus thousands of others).

What's Really In This Book
(Almost "R" Rated Ergonomics)

Presented here are jobs (and more) where real Ergonomics would never have been thought to be found. Although difficult to believe, these are real jobs performed by real people with real occupational injuries involving:

- Turkey Jerking
- Strip Joints
- Elephant Plop Hauling
- Adult Toy Factories

Caution – if you do not have a sense of humor, are exceptionally uptight or are offended by risqué events or sayings, it is strongly recommended you read something else.

If you continue to read, remember these are not fictional fantasies, but real people, trying to earn an honest living doing…hmmm…what shall we say unorthodox jobs.

- **The projects are real**
- **The applications are real**
- **The solutions are real**

These jobs and stories are presented here because they are funny, almost preposterous and generally can't be talked about in professional worker compensation circles. I hope you laugh and enjoy them.

Introduction

Ergonomics is perhaps one of the most misunderstood and misused concepts in business lexicon. **There are many "Ergonomic" things out there, including, chairs, keyboards, mice, coffee pots, pencils, knives, dog toys, bras, jock straps and yes, even sex toys**. The word "Ergonomic" has unfortunately evolved into becoming a simple marketing adjective used by those who would say or do anything to sell their product to those unaware.

There are also continual countless applications of "bad", pretend or kindergarten variety (voodoo) Ergonomics attempting to address occupational pain. These outlandish blunders have left a swath of workers still in pain without any solution in sight. Bad Ergonomics is really a bad thing, especially when it happens to <u>you</u>.

"Bad or Voodoo Ergonomics" became a true inspiration for these writings. Without having witnessed so much first hand, I would never have been moved to present Ergonomics at a deeper, more meaningful level.

Needless to say, some bawdy humor resulted here, not because occupational injuries are not the sexiest of subjects, but because these stories are simply so outrageous that the humor simply exists.

With the almost "R" rated factor (be assured that all stories are all true), I present the Art of Ergonomics which will undoubtedly someday have a grand effect on you or someone you know or love. I'm sure you will never look at Ergonomics the same way again.

Ergonomics just doesn't have to do with selling chairs, making a bent handle or the design of a car interior. It has a lot to do with occupational injuries, making safer more productive workstations or work tasks, reducing chance of industrial injury. ***Most of all it has to do with taking away people's pain.***

Ergonomics can save people's jobs and livelihoods by enabling them to continue working to support their families. It has also saved companies countless dollars in improved performance and productivity with insightful solutions.

Real Ergonomics deals with real issues with real occupational injuries, and is not just advertising fluff.

Following are examples of really outrageous Real Ergonomics in areas you wouldn't think possible, applied in taking away people's pain and allowing them to keep their jobs and support their families.

Please read with an open mind and think of the REAL POTENTIAL offered by the science.

Table of Contents

Ergo Scene I

The Turkey Jerkers

Ever wondered how eggs get fertilized? Did you know that a fertilized egg has more protein than a non-fertilized egg? Those on a health kick should know this.

Now in the quest for higher productivity, performance, attainment and efficiency, artificial insemination has been introduced to the turkey industry...and so has Ergonomics.

The Story

One of my most memorable experiences as an Ergonomist was in a turkey factory/farm. You know, where they raise turkeys and then disassemble the turkeys into parts for Thanksgiving, summer barbeques, turkey soup...you get the idea.

Well being a young hotshot Ergonomist I thought I knew a lot about bringing a turkey to market. I mean, how difficult could it be? You feed it, you take it to the big house and there it becomes food. Well, there just happened to be one minor detail to turkey factories that I didn't know existed. You see, in order to process turkeys, you also need to create them. My assignment was to address this particular area of turkey procreation and to diminish the pain experienced by workers involved with this highly specialized task.

There I was, out in a turkey farm in my three-piece suit and brand new Florsheim shoes. If you have ever been on a turkey farm, you know how they smell and feel. Especially memorable is the fact you are walking in about four inches of turkey plop. On top of that, these ugly turkeys peck at your legs and feet while you navigate your way through the herd, troupe, flock, cacophony or whatever you call a bunch of turkeys.

About 50 yards yonder working in a shed was a group of women. On the wall of the shed was a HUGE Sign showing a high level of worker camaraderie and self esteem which read in big bold letters:

"We're the Turkey Jerkers"

Agatha

The shed was about 20 feet x 20 feet with about 5 or 6 tables in the middle. One specific woman (let's call her Agatha) was standing at one of the tables with her back to the door and holding up a turkey in her left arm, much like a mother would hold a child one handed. I couldn't exactly see what she was doing with the other hand. Meanwhile all these turkeys were in what appeared to be a line similar in shape and activity of a group of rock fans surrounding a booth for a famous rock band, on Agatha's left side.

Upon closer scrutiny and query, Agatha showed me EXACTLY what she was doing. She was…well, masturbate___ the turkey... Uh, before we go on, first a little background. In order to grow turkeys, you need eggs. Not only eggs, but fertilized eggs. And there was traditionally only one way to fertilize eggs. Yes, you guessed it. They (the turkey farmers) would put a Tom turkey in a pen with a bunch of Hen turkeys and let him do his thing.

And like most males during the mating ritual, after mounting the Hen, during the throes of ecstasy, the Tom's feet would pulsate, gyrate and otherwise kick wildly out of control. And since Tom turkeys have the long talons, these throes of ecstasy would negatively impact the Hen's breast meat, which is the most prime cut of turkey meat (the cut that the turkey growers sell for delicacies at the highest price). Scarred up breast meat just doesn't sell well and the farmers wanted intact breast meat.

To combat the clawing of the Tom turkey in ecstasy, conventional thinking at the time developed small canvas "flak" jackets to be tied around the Hens. When tied tightly, these were found to work reasonably well in keeping the Tom's talons from contacting the Hen's breast meat. But these little "flak" jackets would often get tangled up around the Hen's neck. You got a fertilized egg, but you also got a dead Hen…not good. The farmers didn't like this very much.

The skill was in masturbat....err "milking" is the politically correct term. Agatha would ...err..."milk" each Tom and when Tom exploded in ecstasy, Agatha would mop up the "essence" off her latex gloves, place it in a sterile test tube, cork it, write the date and store it in the refrigerator under the table.

The funniest thing about this is when Agatha was done with Tom; she would set him down on the floor…and **Get This**, *Tom would immediately scurry around the table and try to get back in line for Agatha to pick him up again for another "milking."*

This is one of the hardest things to explain to anyone. I'm watching this and it looks completely absurd. I wish I had a video of this. To top it off, when the recently "done" Toms circled the table, they would try to cut in line. Naturally, it was always the biggest and meanest Tom that bullied his way to the front, where Agatha, who appeared totally oblivious to the whole thing would simply pick him up again, and try to "milk" him again. After all, who wouldn't want to be "milked" again?

Real Repetitive Motion Injuries

Well, I don't know about you, but according to Masters and Johnson, most people need a little recuperation after a bout of ecstasy otherwise there is no payload on the second go around. So unbeknownst to Agatha, she would reach down and pick up the same Tom and she would pump and pump and pump and nothing would happen. What does she do? Agatha keeps pumping and develops a dreaded Repetitive Motion Injury (RMI) from repetitive turkey jerking. Like many an occupational injury, too much repeated motion over a lengthy time period and Whammo! you've got pain, numbness and tingling, which is what happened with Agatha. She and some of her co-workers were in real distress. Their jobs were being affected by the repetitive motion work tasks.

Like all good young analysts, I had to analyze this work task and determine specifically the muscle group and biomechanical motion involved. This would allow me to develop some sort of solution to get poor Agatha and her colleagues out of pain and back to work jerking…err, milking…oh, you know what I mean.

Agatha gave me a white lab coat, which I donned over my three-piece suit, being slightly overdressed in that environment. I got help with a hairnet over my coiffure. I put on a pair of latex gloves. My new Florsheim shoes needed replacing with rubber boots. And I proceeded to "milk" the next Tom in line, making sure he wasn't the last one "done." Agatha assured me he wasn't.

Although I couldn't understand how she could tell. I guess this knowledge comes with time: after all she is quite experienced at this.

Can you imagine how I felt? In my three piece suit, and my brand new Florsheims, an 18 pound turkey under my left arm and rapidly pushing and pulling on Tom's manliness while he just stays there soaking it all in.

It was an experience never forgotten and indescribably absurd!

Left Arm Problems

On top of all the right hand and wrist trauma, the Ladies' left shoulder and biceps structures were constantly on fire. Think about it. If you were holding up an 18-25 pound load of firewood all day long, your shoulder and arm would be on fire too.

Holding up a live turkey is almost the same as a bunch of dead firewood, since the turkeys don't really want to move except maybe for little bit of squirming and turkey style moaning…but for the most part these big feathery things are just dead weight with continual static loading on the girls upper arm and shoulder.

Solution

On to a solution for poor Agatha…and by the way I
had to make sure the work task did not lose any
productivity, so I had to keep Tom's satisfaction in
mind. I racked my brain for a solution, which wasn't
easy since all my experience, all my schooling and all
my creative brainpower had not even remotely
prepared me for this project.

In complete desperation, I called some of my
colleagues whose input and work I respected, asking if
they had any ideas. Four phone calls and all I got was
endless laughter on the phone in between choking
phrases of "You're doing WHAT????
HAHAHAHAHAHAHAHAHAHAHA!!!!!!!!!!!!!!!!!!!"

Pink Pussycat Adult Boutique

Like a dutiful analyst, I did my research, developed an
approach, got in my car and drove to the nearest big
city looking for a specialty shop and so found the Pink
Pussycat Adult Boutique. I walked in the door still
dressed in my 3 piece suit and Florsheim shoes.
Almost everyone inside was dressed de rigueur in
black leather including Rene, the guy behind the
counter. I sauntered past all the displays, videos, and
other "recreational" paraphernalia to one of the glass
merchandise counters and began my research by
evaluating the displays.

Along comes Rene dressed in very, very tight black leather pants (so tight, you could tell if he had a nickel or dime in his pocket) tucked into black motorcycle boots. No shirt, just red suspenders with a nametag "Rene." Oh yes, he had piercings in all bodily extremities that I could see. No tats that I remember.

"Can I help you?" he asks merrily.

"Yeah, sure, I want to look at your vibrators."

"Well, we have lots of different kinds" he says, and begins by opening the counter backside sliding door and bringing them out one by one, and lining them up neatly on a black velvet pad atop the glass countertop.

"We have the regular kind."
"We have the gold ones."
"We have silver ones."
"We have clear ones."
"We have colored ones."
"We have the kinds that have texture on them."
"Of course all of these come in different sizes."

"Of course" I acknowledged.

"We have the kind that light up."
"We have the kind that move in circles."
"And we just got these, these are really cool, they make sounds."

"Well thanks, but I just need the regular type like these", incidating the first kind Rene brought out.

"Ok", says Rene and begins to neatly line them up back inside the glass display case. "That'll be $7.98 plus tax."

"I need a bunch of them", I told Rene.

"How many"?

"Well, let's see", making mental calculations: 8 Jerkers on shifts & weekends, allowing for breakdown, extras, etc. "I think I need an even two dozen", I said thoughtfully.

"Two dozen????? Goodness Gracious! What are you going to use that many for?" exclaims Rene.

"Don't ask", I winked back.

"Oh I see", he returned my wink.

"Well if you need that many, I'll have to go in the back and get a case."

Rene goes in the back and I hear some rustling around, like boxes being moved. Out comes another guy, dressed exactly like Rene, except the nametag on his red suspenders says "Richard."

Richard places a box of vibrators on the counter top and with a big smile enthusiastically grabs my hand over the glass counter top and in a lively action shakes my hand enwrapped in both of his, exclaiming quite loudly "I just wanted to shake your hand, I've never sold anyone a WHOLE CASE of vibrators at once before!" Everyone else in the boutique looked at me and gave me knowing smiles or started giggling.

"What are you going to use so many for?" Richard inquired.

"Don't ask" I winked back for the second time.

"Oh,......I seeeeee" he said in a singsong manner. "That'll be 24 times 7.98 and since you're buying a WHOLE case, we'll give you a 10% discount". The cash register lit up, "You'll need batteries of course."

"Of course", I replied enthusiastically.

"Use the Eveready" Richard recommended. "They last longer than the Duracell."

"How do you know?" I asked.

"Don't ask", he winked back at me.

"I see", I replied thoughtfully.

With all my new purchases in hand, I traveled back to the Turkey Jerker field house. "What are these?" the girls giggled (as if they didn't know).

"Here, let me show you how to do it."

"Wowowowow, these really work neat, no hand action required", they squealed happily.

The turkeys loved it (who wouldn't). The gals loved it, no hand action required, and all wrist pain eliminated. All at-risk postures and conditions eliminated.

Everyone was very thankful to the Ergonomist in the new Florsheim shoes.

I thought I had done an exemplary job – Not Quite!!!

Battery Problems

I made a site review a few months later. One of the foremen called me over and told me the "girls" would like to see me. "What about?" I inquired. "Dunno, just said if I see you, to send you over", he said. "OK."

When I got to the field house, I looked up Agatha. She was very pleased to see me because she and all the other Jerkers were back to manually "milking" the Tom Turkeys. I asked why? Agatha informed me the batteries ran out and the purchaser wouldn't get them any new ones. "How come?" "Don't know only that our request for batteries got shut down."

OK. I went to see the purchaser to plead the case for more batteries. The purchaser was a new guy, Bill, I knew him in passing. "Hi Bill, can we get some more batteries for the Gals out in the field house?" Being new, I didn't know if he knew what Jerkers were.

"Not really", he responded.

"Why not?"

"Look, there are several things that we can't just go off supplying to everyone Willie Nillie. You know things that have a high theft index. Things like Cross Pens, yellow pads during school sessions, leather notebook portfolios, you know things that disappear a lot. We have a company policy to help prevent a lot of theft. Perhaps a one-time supply, but you're on your own after that. Batteries fall into this category. Sorry, can't help you. What are you using so many batteries for anyway?"

So I told him in great detail. "Oh No", he sadly exclaimed while covering his eyes with his hands and tilting his head back. "You're doing WHAT???"

Look, I can plumb you power, I can get you air, I can get you electricity, But I'm sorry, I can't get you any more batteries, what would my boss think?"

Your boss is interested in getting his turkeys "milked" I thought to myself.

"No, no, no, no-No…..No more batteries."

I had to regroup. What to do? What to do?

Back to the Pink Pussycat

I got back in my car and headed back to see Rene; surely he could help me out. I walked in, still in a suit, and Rene looked up and exclaimed loudly and with glee, "I REMEMBER YOU, you're, you're……you're the one who bought the whole case of vibrators." Everyone in the place looked around at me, I blushed. "Is there anything wrong with them?" quizzed Rene. "We have a money back guarantee."

"Yeah, who's going to want to use them after I'm done with them", I thought to myself.

"No" I said, "everything's fine. I just need an upgrade."

"An upgrade?"

"Yeah, an upgrade. It seems the batteries are running out, need constant replacing and I have to address that issue."

"Batteries running out" exclaimed Rene incredulously. "Did you buy the Energizers that Richard recommended?" They are better than the Duracells you know. How long are you using them anyway?" He asked.

"Let's see. About 8 hours a shift", I replied.

"8 hours a shift!?" The response came with a puzzled look, which then evolved to a slight turning of the head, a lowering of the eyelids and a low breathless whisper. " Oh My, WE… are… a…. stud aren't we?"

"No, no, not really, I just need something that doesn't need batteries."

"Well", Rene says thoughtfully. "We have the kind that plugs into a wall outlet, if that'll work for you."

"Sure, let me see them."

"They plug into a wall with a low voltage step down, like your calculator plug, with the little black box that plugs into an outlet. They're quite safe for use in moist environments."

"Oh really?"

"Oh yes, and these also come in gold, silver, textured, colors and…"

"Never mind, I just need some of the regular kind."

"With variable speed?" Rene asked matter-of-factly.

"Oh yes with variable speeds", thinking of the "Girls."

"You'll want a case, right?"

"Right!"

Richard wasn't around, otherwise I could have said goodbye.

Well, I got the new vibrators back to Agatha and friends and distributed them accordingly. I didn't even need Bill to install some new wiring. I just used the outlets they had previously installed for the refrigerators.

To eliminate the shoulder pain when the Jerkers continually held up a heavy turkey with the left arm we built small platforms, adjustable height of course, like art pedestals. The Girls could then just rest the turkeys on top of the platforms without the need to continually carry the weight.

I've often been asked, "Did the turkeys stay on the pedestals?" Well, just think about it, they are having the time of their lives being "milked" by someone. Would you go anywhere?

We also installed colored neck rings to show that the "blue" turkeys were "milked" at 2 o'clock and the green ones at 3 o'clock and the red ones at 4. We also quarantined off the interior of the field shack with low fences keeping all the blues separate from the reds and so on for accurate count. Simple logistics and methods applications here combined for good Ergonomics, just like a good Kaizan or Kan Ban project.

Last I heard, Agatha and her friends had a lot less pain, could "milk" more turkeys without worrying about how long they could last in this job. Like most other workers they were in an aging group and the worktasks were obviously taking their toll. Their job was just as important to them as yours is to you. In reality, they were well trained, highly paid and took great pride in what they do, just like most of us.

When I paid my last follow-up to Agatha, she profusely thanked me and gave me a big smile, telling me that what we do as Ergonomists is really great in helping people keep their jobs and that it must be very rewarding. Yes it is. She also asked me what to do with all the extra battery powered vibrators.

I dunno, maybe E-Bay?

Ergo Scene II

The Strip Joint Story

Believe it or not exotic dancing also has its occupational injuries. Dancers get injured just like the typical factory worker or computer jockey.

Here you will see exotic dancing in a totally different light and how Ergonomic applications really work.

The Story

What mental picture does the term "strip joint" trigger in your mind? In my mind, as an Ergonomist, it naturally just means another occupation where injuries occur. Right? Riiiiiiiiiight!!

As I progressed through my career, and dealing with any type of occupational injury folks could throw my way, I came across some really fun and interesting ones. Some seem so surreal, that when I perform the analysis, develop a solution and execute the workplan, all the while thinking, "This is really bizarre." Like the turkey story, this one falls into my "Ergonomics of the Absurd" hall of fame.

Dancers

We got a call, not too long ago. It wasn't much different from all the other calls our firm gets when someone needs some help regarding occupational injuries. An utterly charming and sweet voice on the other end inquired if we could help get her "injuries more Ergonomically designed." Kind of an odd way of saying things, but we've heard that type of verbiage before. It usually indicates that the caller, while not being fully cognizant about the science of Ergonomics, is at least in the beginnings of research on how to get some help.

"Sure we can help," I replied. "What kind of injuries do your folks have? "

"One knee injury and one back injury. We're trying to see if there is anything Ergonomically we can do to prevent other injuries. We're very concerned about our workers and we're trying to be very proactive."

Naturally, I replied, "You're doing the right thing and I bet your workers are very much in favor of this."

"Oh yes" she said enthusiastically. "In fact they were the ones who really wanted to do something about injury prevention. So…can you tell me how your firm does a project?"

"Be happy to," I replied. "First we do an on-site analysis of the worktasks and determine the causal relationship to the injuries. Then we work with the injured workers and management to formulate an acceptable plan for workstation modification. Most of all, our firm has the unique capability to design, construct, install any workstation modification, tools, equipment or whatever is required. We also hold training workshops when needed. **But most important is for our analysts to actually perform the job during the onsite, to actually get a feel on the causal relationship of the task to the injuries.** Usually we come out with cameras, video, measuring tools, dress in work clothes ***and perform the job of injury,*** to determine the specific anatomical structures that are being affected. Since most people have a bit of difficulty describing specific symptomology, it is best that our analysts actually feel it to determine exactly what is happening biomechanically.

We do this at the initial onsite analysis. Does that answer your question?"

"Yes, it's very clear. Another question,.....do you have any experience with dancers?

At this point, I lapsed into professional fantasy. "Now what kind of dance troupe would actually entertain hiring an Ergonomics consultant to help their dancers?" I asked myself. Then it dawned on me. Of course, it had to be, like an unexpected gift from the Ergonomics gods, the **City Ballet Troupe**. I could be the Ergonomist for the CBT. How exciting...think how that would look on our professional portfolio. But wait, who else could be in the Ergonomics market? Aha!. Maybe the **Alvin Ailey** group, another coup for our Ergonomics expertise. Surely this was going to be a high visibility project, doing something for a high level cultural entity. To have our firm associated with such class, such erudite society, some real "Haute Couture." This was an opportunity not to be mishandled. I was dead set on turning in the most professional and expert presentation I knew how to lasso this project. Not only was our firm's livelihood at stake, but the prospect of doing something that hasn't been done before and to contribute to the cultural arts in a manner that we were considered expert was an opportunity not to be squandered. I was excited, I was salivating, and I was nervous with anticipation.

I gathered in my most professional demeanor, and tried to reply in the most professional and knowledgeable voice. "Well, as a firm, we've never had a dance troupe project before. Personally, I have had experience with dancers. We studied them extensively in Ergonomics school. Many of my classmates in the curriculum were dancers studying kinesiology, physiology and human performance. We were taught to think of the dancers using the body as a tool… much like a mechanics tool, but using the body. The body requires special handling, care, maintenance and utmost respect one would offer an expensive, valuable and irreplaceable piece of equipment. The approach of care biomechanically and Ergonomically is the same.

I continued to explain our professional philosophy. "The principles and approach of taking care of the body related to task performance (the human body doing something) are quite simple, you just require an in-depth knowledge of the human anatomy, since we are dealing with only the human body being the tool (of expression, in this case). Great care must be given not to exceed certain limits of motion, force and usage, much like any other tool. The limits must be adhered to preventing the risk of the tool or body to fail, in which case you have an injury.

The pleasant voice on the phone said, "I appreciate the way you approach dancers, and what you say makes a lot of sense. I think it would help a great deal if our dancers kind of knew what to do in not exceeding their, how did you put it…. anatomical limits?

"Yes, that's right, not exceeding these limits will have a big impact in injury prevention during task performance, or in your case dancing. It also means your dancers will probably be able to perform longer in their career since they're placing less overall stress on their anatomy."

She then asked, "Can you come down and take a look at our operation and tell us how you might approach this? We've called all over and really haven't found anyone else who even remotely thinks they can help. Perhaps some training of some sort? I know the dancers would really welcome some outside input on warm-ups and that sort of thing."

I was elated. I could see our company name and logo associated with a cultural icon. I felt like I had moved our firm up on the professional ladder. "Sure where are you located?" I asked, opening my appointment calendar.

"Uptown" was the reply.

The Uptown Professional Dance Troupe

I could feel my brows furrow. I could feel my mind instantaneously go into puzzlement. "Uptown?" I thought. Let's see. The City Ballet Troupe is by the Theater District, and the last time I saw Alvin Ailey, they were holding workshops in one of the local Universities. So who's this pleasant voice on the other end of the phone that I've just committed an analysis to? I just couldn't picture any dance troupe in the Uptown. And then, like a flash, it came to me.

"Are you...Are you...uh... I stammered.

"Yes, we're the Show Time Revue" (not the real name) was the reply. "So what does your schedule look like for next week?"

As you can imagine, and as the name implies, it is a "men's" club, peep show, skin flick type of operation. It has a very good reputation around town for several reasons. The dancers are employees and are covered under the standard worker compensation insurance for industrial injuries.

They even have benefits: sick leave, vacations and the conditions are quite good. Our firm has an open office environment. We believe in approaching projects as a team, feeling that no one Ergonomist - no matter how smart, highly educated or skilled - has a lock on brains. Therefore, all of our activity, including phone calls, notes, etc is the open property of all.

When I mentioned The Show Time Revue, all heads turned in my direction. All male hands immediately went up, straining in the air, much like a young second grader who knows the answer and really, really, reeeaaaaly wants to tell the teacher. It seems a lot of folks wanted to do that analysis.

Riiiiiiiiiggggggggghhhhhhtttttttt guys, "Where were you when I needed some help photographing that sewer cleaning operations last week when I was up to my waist in sewage glop? Or how about the other day when I had to go analyze the lifting operations at Animal Control while they were disposing their entire collected road kill. Where were you then? Oh I remember, you were getting a root canal or taking your cat to be groomed. UmmmmHmmmmm. No, I think I might force myself to do this project."

Angel

The charming voice on the phone was Angel (stage name) who was the office manager and my main contact, the top client in consulting jargon.

Angel was a very charming and very attractive young lady - very business-like and like most good managers, appeared to really care about her dancers. We talked at length on what could or couldn't be done, what approaches could be used and some of my preliminary thoughts regarding the stage, the dancers themselves and a training program.

After a quick tour of the facilities and introductions to the dancers on shift, Angel asked how I would like to begin. Following the advice of the dancers who thought I should actually observe the real conditions of their routines (which is exactly what we do in observing workers actually performing their worktasks). Angel led me to a booth and supplied me with a cupful of coins to insert into the electronic screen to watch the "girls" as she affectionately called them.

Research

Having done my research and looking back at the project, I can safely say that many peep show venues are quite similar. Mostly, they have small phone booth size booths for viewing movie clips or for watching the live show. For movies, just step in, lock the door, insert a coin and choose from a keypad one of several flicks that strikes your fancy. Viewing time varies from venue to venue, at about 30 seconds per coin. Normally, you have to supply your own coins.

The live action booths are small, with a coin slot and an opaque window that looks out onto a raised stage. Insert a coin and the high-tech window electronically turns transparent. In the old days, there was a double pane of glass with a roll up window shade in between. Roll up action occurs when a coin was inserted. Roll down occurs when the timer runs out.

How do I know all this? In a past professional life, I had opportunity to actually work on a men's club project in another of the big cities. It dawned on me at that time, that Ergonomics could transcend any occupation since I saw a lot of shortcomings and areas in which the dancers and patrons could benefit from the application of good sound Ergonomics practices. Perhaps that experience prepared me for this particular project (unlike the companion Turkey Jerker Story) and maybe it's a trend in my professional career. But that would be another tale.

Bump & Grind

So, Angel left me in the booth with my cup of coins so I could observe the girls under "battle" conditions. I watched the girls bump and gyrate for a while to see how they used the stage and position themselves in front of the other patron's electronic windows. A couple of the girls, to whom I had been introduced, decided I needed some special treatment and began to get a little frisky and give me a special "show."

"No, no, no, no, NO!" I replied while I rolled my eyes and shook my head. "I just want to watch you do what you do under normal circumstances. No goofing off, no special shows, no special good behavior and no acrobatics, just show me what you normally do.

So after some playfulness, they got down to the business of entertainment dancing. From behind the now transparent window, I watched them perform their acts and noticed a major comparison to dancers I had studied way back in school. The common element was balance is a most important element when doing an extreme move or trying out a new routine.

I stayed in my booth until I was satisfied my knowledge of their worktasks was satiated. It was time to get into the stage area and do some inspection and analysis. I was looking forward to this.

I went around the back and into the performer's entrance and entered the raised stage area. The stage was typical of men's club performance. Red shag carpet naturally, a multitude of colored theatrical lights, a single dancers pole (vertical) and a back wall completely covered by mirror.

After taking some measurements of the stage and booth layout, I dove right into my analysis. The conversation went something like this:

"Show me how you stay in that position." I would ask.

"It's really easy, once you get used to it. It also really helps if you are in shape (hint, hint) like most of the girls here."

"Doesn't it hurt when you do that?"

"No, we can usually tell when we've reached our limits with these various positions and make sure we don't over do it. Because, if we do and we strain something, we're off work." Naturally there are some positions we would love to perform to keep the patrons coming back, putting in their coins or for tips.

"Like what positions?"

"Like these."

"That looks difficult to do."

"No, it's fairly easy. Here let me show you how to do it."

"Gee, that's not so bad."

"It's only bad when you don't know your own limitations or you don't have anything to grab for support. Here try and hold this position. Yes, yes, that's it, you look great."

"I can feel a few things straining," I grimaced.

"No it's OK. Just balance yourself on this dancer's pole. See? It's really easy. Now the hard part is to adjust the viewing angle of yourself so the patron in the booths can see "your goods.""

"My goods?"

"Yes, you know, your goods."

"Look girls, isn't our Ergonomist cute? Heeheeheehee."

Just then a patron put in a coin and before any of the girls could react to perform for him, the window turned transparent and he got a full view of me entangled upon the dancer's pole. Naturally all of the girls giggled. I turned red. The patron made a hasty exit out the booth and out the front door. I knew right then, that my career, as an exotic dancer was limited at best.

As my fantasies being an exotic dancer evaporated in the stage lighting, I turned to the task at hand, especially since I couldn't properly orient myself towards the patron to effectively show off my "goods."

"See what we mean?" one of the dancers offered, "We can get the correct sight lines to some of these booths from this one dancer pole. And on top of that this is the only place on stage where we can actually balance ourselves to do some of the more erotic moves."

Real Occupational Injuries

"You know some of the girls have minor injuries that aren't even reported," added another. "We just deal with them, let them heal on their own and try not to do the things that cause the injuries."

"So you've got some minor injuries commonly occurring?" I inquired.

"Yes, but they're really nothing we can't live with and certainly not career threatening, just continually aggravating."

"What sort of minor issues?"

"You know small ankle twists, slights sprains, a minor strain of leg or back muscle."

She added "But the ones you know about, the knee and back occur because there's simply nothing to hang on to for balance. The result is a slip when you don't know it's coming, especially when we are leaning on the mirror facing the booths. The hot stage lights make us sweat and there isn't enough friction on the mirror when we lean against it and keep our back up, especially when we're wearing high heels. And on that shag carpet, well, the footing isn't the greatest and we're always worried about slipping down and injuring ourselves."

Ergo Scene II - The Strip Joint Story

So finally clues began to emerge for a solution for the girls' problems. Sweat on the mirror, bad footing with stiletto heels on shag carpet and nothing to grab hold of when secure balance is needed. Well, the shag carpet had to stay. Even if it wasn't shag, any surface with stiletto heels was bad, especially keeping the feet about 18 inches in front of the mirror and squatting in a semi-seated position to show off the "goods" was bad. Oh yes, the stiletto heels had to stay, part of the mystique of this type of industry, you know.

Another occupational injury expressed by the girls was the problem of neck strain. A little puzzled, I inquired "neck strain?"

"Yes, neck strain."

"Just how do you get neck strain while you are dancing?" I certainly didn't observe any movements and postures up on stage that would have a causal relationship to neck strain.

"No no, these occur when we're dancing in front of the booths for "special shows," came a multi-voiced reply.

"Special shows?" I thought aloud.

"Yeah, when the patrons want a little extra, we dance right on the other side of the window so they can get a real good view of us." And that naturally comes along with a better tip.

"So how does that trigger neck strain." I kept inquiring.

"Well, the window is at eye level for the patrons in the booth and about 18" high. And since we're up on stage, the window hits us between hips and neck. To really connect with the patron, we do a lot of eye contact, you know, demurely and intensely looking into their eyes while were performing for them, so they can get the full view.

"Full view huh?" I had to think and gave a, what I thought, typical male voyeur response. "Look, I'm a guy right?" I said to the gathering, "and if I'm coming in here to watch, I'm looking at the areas between the neck and thighs. I don't know if I'm really interested in *EYE CONTACT*"

"Yeah you are," they replied emphatically, "and the more eye contact and "relationship" we have with the patrons, the more they stay or come back. And to keep this eye contact we have to lower our head and stretch our neck forward, with our shoulders back and hips forward so they can get the full view."

"Right, and keeping our bodies like this without anything to hang onto makes our necks really sore. And boy, do we need a massage around our shoulders and neck all the time, these muscles are always really tight, especially in these high heels, our backs are curved and our necks take a real punishment. We could really use something to hang onto in front of the booth windows - something to help eliminate the balance issues and reduce the chances of the common minor injuries. It seems that if anything were done, it would benefit the dancers a lot."

In approaching these dancers as athletes, which I feel they are, one can look past their occupational worktasks and appreciate how much "in shape" they really are to attain the various positions and perform the routines they do.

The Solutions / Workplan

I reached way down into the depths of my Ergonomics training and visualized a ballerina's balance bar attached to the walls in front of the mirrors. Installing one of these would give the girls a secure handhold while they perform in various positions. Adding another strategically located vertical dancer's pole would also help the girls with balance and with the all-important positioning of themselves with appropriate sight lines for the patrons. High friction soles for the high heels were also retrofitted as part of the program to help stabilize footing.

Balance was the key. Balance was also needed when performing in front of the booth windows. A simple set of grab bars appeared to be a successful solution. One horizontal bar over the window and two vertical ones, on either side of window would provide more than adequate hand holds for the girls and allow them to take different positions without straining their neck and upper back musculatures.

One of the last implementations was introducing some stretching and toning techniques the girls could use in the back room during breaks before and after their shift. A large stretching ball and hanging trapeze were the items the girls felt were needed. Our expertise justified the need for these and the approach for management approval.

Concluding Thoughts About the Troupe's Solution

When you really think about it, the solutions are quite simple, just figure out what the problem is and place in something that takes away the problem.

The real hard part is determining what the problem is. But in fact, it is quite easy when you think about it...all you have to do is just ask the workers. We did it at Show Time and the solutions came about directly from their input and some articulation by us.

We were glad to help them. In addition to the stage area design, we held some training workshops for all the girls to explain some basic biomechanics, body positioning and how not to stress their bodies. In turn they promised to teach me some exotic dance routines that would no doubt skyrocket my career as a dancer if I ever wanted to give up the Ergonomics profession.

Additional Concluding Thoughts

This was a real project. In working with the dancers, I got to talk with them and got to know them a little. Many were students at one of the local Universities. Some just danced for the income. Others were also pursuing or trying to develop careers in the performing dance profession. All were concerned about their body as a tool and its limitations regarding movement, injury and most of all longevity.

Theirs is undoubtedly a unique profession, being involved with it, much like you probably are with yours. Being Ergonomists, we have to respect that profession and the workers in it. To not do so is a disservice to our profession and to those we are hired to help. During presentations, I have had people leave the audience in a huff upon finding out I have practiced Ergonomics in this area. I wonder why. It is a real profession with real injuries. Why are you getting so snooty and feel you can't face someone who has helped someone continue their job, profession or career? It often amazes me that these people think, "That's not real Ergonomics." Yes it is, and they shouldn't try to make it elitist. It's a science that should be practiced to help everyone from the most humble of professions to those requiring much skill, education and unique performance. The human body is susceptible to injuries in all professions and it is indeed a blessing to be able to help the workers no matter what the work tasks or how injuries occur.

Ergo Scene III.

Shoveling Elephant Plop
Yes, Elephant Plop

A zookeeper with a back injury from shoveling elephant plop cannot continue his zoo keeping work duties, such as: well….shoveling elephant plop. So why is shoveling elephant plop more prone to injury than shoveling horse plop, dog plop or even rabbit plop?

Well, for one thing, there's more of it, a lot more, and it's a lot heavier and never deposited in a convenient place. It's usually way out in the far reaches of the elephant exhibit tundra.

If you have ever manipulated a 200 pound wheelbarrow full of wet cement you can fully appreciate the problems here. Even just hitting a small pothole in your garden with a wheelbarrow full of garden debris can give you a basic idea of the difficult issues handling an unstable load over rough terrain. Add a real stench and you get the picture. Ergonomics is definitely the answer!

The Story

This inquiry came from the city zoo. The zoo is a wonderful place...sooo interesting because it has so many unusual areas where Ergonomics can benefit not only the zookeepers but the animals too.

This particular inquiry dealt with a zookeeper who had a back injury. Not uncommon in an area where a lot of manual labor is performed. Our first question was "What was he lifting? After a long pause with giggling, the answer was elephant plop. Well we've never had anyone complain about hauling rabbit plop, or horse plop or any other kind of plop, so why is elephant plop so special in causing injuries.

Well, it just happens (taken from our conversation) that there is usually a lot; I mean a lot more elephant plop than rabbit, horse or any other kind of plop. Just think about it. The amount of plop is obviously directly proportional to the size of the animal.

Additionally, when an elephant drinks too much water or eats the wrong kind of peanuts, the plop becomes, well, increasingly less solid and it gets heavier, just like wet snow. When your are shoveling this stuff, it's difficult…particularly if you already have a disk ready to rupture, a muscle that's ready to strain or a ligament that's ready to stretch, an injury can occur. It's the same when an out of shape couch potato goes out at winter's first snowfall and tries to clear the driveway to get the family car out. That is the most common complaint in emergency rooms around the country during Old Man Winter's White Christmas.

The other contributing factor about elephant plop is that it has to be gathered from the exhibition plains. In current state-of-the-art cutting edge zoos, animals like elephants are no longer just held in cages. They roam in large areas of rough terrain to replicate some of the natural environment, both for animals and viewers. These exhibit plains are sometimes very large, and elephant plop needs to be periodically cleared from the far reaches of the exhibit areas. The (un) Ergonomic tools are usually a shovel, rake, broom, hoe and standard single wheel, solid tire, second class lever type wheelbarrow. You know, the kind we've all seen in movies, in hardware stores or you might even own a rusted out model, the kind with the wooden handles and big metal hopper or tray.

clkr,cim

Inadequate Tools

These types of wheelbarrows with the single wheel use a second-class lever principle forcing the zookeeper to hold up roughly one half of the load when he picks up the wheelbarrow after filling it (with the wheel holding the other half) and maneuver it over rough terrain. This usually without the benefit of a pneumatic wheel which would make the job much easier. The poor zookeeper is already behind the eight ball since he has just shoveled some heavy loads on a typical (un) Ergonomic shovel and with an inefficient wheelbarrow must undergo some dangerous and at-risk maneuvering of a heavy wheelbarrow over dirt, rocks, crevices, ridges, without spilling any of his wet elephant plop.

If any of you have worked with a heavy single wheeled wheelbarrow, you know how difficult it is. Especially with a bad back, shoulder or hip acting up.

Serious gardeners know exactly what I mean. If you've ever moved a heavy 200 pound wheelbarrow full of wet cement when you were re-casting your patio walk or driveway, you also know exactly what I mean. Thus you have a recipe of at-risk conditions ready to trigger an injury. And this is what happened. Elephant plop conditions were directly responsible.

The Solution

Elephant diapers were one of the many brainstorming ideas presented to the worker comp powers that be. However it wasn't exactly viewed as very creative and not exactly in spirit of a cutting edge zoo. So we had to regroup and really put our minds towards a real solution.

To move any kind of load using a human powered drag along hay wagon like the really inefficient wheelbarrow is obviously preposterous. There is a new breed of wheelbarrow, which can move a lot of any material including elephant plop with very little effort. They have four wheels, some with pneumatic tires allowing traversing over rough terrain. Some even have suspensions. Moving a loaded single wheel wheelbarrow over rough terrain, I'm sure many of you weekend gardeners know is very difficult. The new models have adjustable height handles allowing each user to set the appropriate height for maximum grip and minimum forward lean and balanced load bearing. They are beautifully designed allowing an easy tilt for unloading, unlike the single wheel type which requires lifting almost the entire load weight in order to dump the load forward.

These are wonderful for any type of material handling. They tilt for dumping, move easily and also are relatively cheap and durable. Highly recommended for any of you professional gardeners, weekend horticulturists or elephant plop movers.

As for shovels…just remember to use a smaller shovel and be careful on how you shovel the …er…..Plop. Don't use an excessively wide unit, try not to get a real heavy load and don't throw it overhead - just lift with appropriate body mechanics. You could even use a bent handled shovel to lift in a more efficient manner with less risk to your back. Think about these things the next time you're shoveling your brand of plop.

Ergo Scene IV.
Adventures in an Adult Toy Factory

Have you ever been in an Adult Toy factory and
retail outlet? Well we have, and it's really an
adventure. We've seen the whole kit and caboodle;
factory, warehouse, distribution, including the
retail sales area.

The Story

The adult toy / fantasy world is undoubtedly unique, requiring at the very least an open mind and most of all a sense of humor.

One of the most interesting things about the folks in this industry is that some of them feel like they are really ambassadors of their world of "avant garde" activities to the real conservative world of less creative lifestyles and are honestly trying to widen perception, acceptance and lateral thinking. I firmly believe that, like many avid folks in a profession they believe in and are dedicated to, that they definitely go out of their way to provide exceptional "customer service" in helping others to have, what shall we say, "a more enlightened, liberated or pleasurable experience in their world." So like most occupations they have their staunch proponents including their share of occupational injuries (also illustrated in our Turkey Jerker and Strip Joint Stories).

So let's start in the beginning and go all the way through to the occupational injuries and safety concerns associated with this intriguing business and profession.

In the Factory

Making adult toys is identical to making any other small plastic or rubber toy or any other small item for that matter. Mostly, manufacturers use typical blow molding, injection molding, insert molding or casting manufacturing techniques; however, it is the psychosocial aspect of these things that make it really interesting.

To begin with, I have been in large toy manufacturing conglomerates where they make dolls. You know, not the "Barbie" type, but the life like, life size ones you or your kid sister played with and even now inhabit vast shelving in major toy and department stores.

There are six major anatomical parts to one of these life size dolls: head, torso, 2 arms and 2 legs. Each is made separately and then ejected from their respective blow molding machine onto a conveyor belt, which transports these parts to a group of assemblers who put all the pieces together to form a doll. Keep in mind these body parts are beautiful flesh colored and there are no painted on eyes, lips, eyebrows yet (these come later) and the pieces are still warm. They simply look like freshly made baby body parts.

This conveyor belt scene is so surreal; it is something out of science fiction. Imagine, if you will, this scene of flesh colored warm baby parts, being ejected from noisy machinery moving slowly past you on a conveyor belt, to be assembled down the line.

They are like real body parts, warm, soft, flesh colored, life size and very life like. You almost feel like if you put them together yourself, it will start squirming and making baby noises, the closest thing to viewing a do-it-yourself baby assembly line. It is truly something out of the SyFy channel and I'm sure someone will or has filmed this to make stunning psychosocial statement.

OK. Now step back and simply think about these same machines making adult appendages. In the medical world, some of these appendages are currently used for breast cancer patients but if you can see in your mind's eye a series of male appendages being ejected from these machines, it is also truly a surreal sight, probably something you will never see on a SyFy channel. On top of that, members of the factory touring group generally pick up assembled baby dolls and remark how life like they are and of course chatter about the science fiction and reality aspects of the assembly line. Interestingly enough, the same cannot be said about the adult toys.

In the Warehouse

An adult toy warehouse is similar to any other warehouse for dry goods. Generally, dark, dank, cold, dusty, rows & rows of high industrial steel shelving, lacking of any amenities of civilization. Always located in some industrial area or out of the way place, often times being an afterthought, placed in a basement of a building, this warehouse was no different.

And like many other warehouses, it has an exhibit of all the products stored and indexed there. And for staff reference, all, and I mean all the products are stuck on a big piece of plywood, hanging out so to speak, showing the appropriate sku number, location of aisle and shelf including other information like manufacturer, box size, weight, etc. You cannot imagine what a sight that is, all these dozens of different types of male appendages mounted and sticking out for (ahem) references.

Imagine dozens of different appendages, all in different colors (natural, clear, pink, red, purple, etc), textures (rough, smooth, semi-smooth, bumps, etc.) sizes (small, medium large, super large, etc.), finishes (chrome, gold) action (spinning, revolving, pulsating, squirting, noisy) all on exhibit in their splendor on this big piece of plywood. It would no doubt elicit some sort of reaction from any viewer. What that reaction would be, I don't know. One of surprise, shock, humor or maybe even anger or disgust. I'm really not sure, but I do know, and I'm sure you do too, that this exhibit couldn't help but draw out some sort of reaction from almost anyone.

This particular warehouse was not on the tour for the general public and for some reason, the warehousemen told me, was that anyone who did come through generally had a bawdy sense of humor and would spend time studying this exhibit, oftentimes accompanied with colorful remarks reflecting humor, disgust or even awe.

One of the concerns of this particular warehouse was the concern from earthquake damage. I'm a firm believer in earthquake preparedness and listened intently. The warehousemen highest fear was what would happen if an earthquake hit and the shelving moved, toppling all of the merchandise into the aisles, trapping them in this basement warehouse. Their utmost fear was that they would be trapped inside without food and water with nothing to eat but sex candy like edible underwear or chocolate thongs (available in both men's and women's styles). EEEWWWWW!!!!! As part of their safety program appropriate food and water were provided in a new survival locker in addition to two way radios, flashlights and batteries. Also implemented was a safety program to reinforce the shelving and to place containment chains across the shelving to keep boxed goods and pallets from being shaken off the shelving and potentially injuring someone or to limit egress to an escape way.

Success with Safety Issues

One of the enterprising warehousemen (and kudos to him) took it upon himself to really address this issue of goods being shaken off the shelving. He knew of a large supply of B&D velvet covered chain link that was discontinued for sale and sitting in the back of the warehoused unused, in pristine condition. He proceeded to use this velvet covered chain to effectively drape across each shelving area to restrain any packaging from being shaken off the shelf in the event of a quake. Using special B&D quick release hardware, he installed these restraining chains throughout the warehouse to the accolades from the boss and safety manager. Not only did his fellow warehousemen feel much safer, and the restraints vastly increased the safety factor in working in the warehouse, but the gold velvet and quick release hardware added a much needed touch of décor (and bawdy sense of humor) to the otherwise drab warehouse atmosphere.

Guess what? Several years later, in a totally unrelated warehouse project, we came across the same scenario. Boxed goods were on shelving and the plant manager was proudly showing us his safety program. He was especially proud of his newly implemented restraining devices for the industrial shelving to prevent the shaking off of goods from the shelving onto the floor with potential injury from an earthquake.

Lo and Behold, the restraining devices were the familiar gold velvet covered chain with the gold quick release hardware. We never did find out who was the actual installer or where he got his inspiration from or indeed where the velvet chain came from. But it was very apparent the plant manager was very proud of the injury prevention these devices provided. The exhibit board was not quite as interesting as the male appendage one, but the velvet covered gold chain link was a definite point of conversation.

On the Retail Side

At the outlet store where we were working, the local utility company was ripping up the street to install some electrical cable. Inside, we found one of the young women we worked with, showing us as part of her job description her duties requiring exemplary customer service. Is selling each of the vibrators, she was to open the box, install the batteries, and test, ensuring each one functioned properly. She did this about 6-8 times per day. Her major concern (relative to industrial injury) was about the amount of vibration she experienced in her hands and whether she would indeed develop some sort of RSI (repetitive strain injury).

Ergo Scene IV - Adult Toy Factory

As part of the new safety program she found interest in the occupational injuries associated with excessive vibration exposure documented in the safety / occupational health trade magazines.

She expressed her concern to us and simply asked if she should wear some of the new vibration damping gloves which absorb nasty vibrations given off by vibrating devices and what kind we would recommend. We performed a bit of analysis and informed her that the vibrations documented were mostly about using vibrating power tools including sanders, grinders and larger tools like the jackhammers used right then and there in the street outside the shop. We educated her on the amplitude, frequency and duration of exposure and even consulted one of our colleagues about such matters, who incidentally broke out laughing at our "research" project, asking how we got involved in such a project. Needless to say, our young lady was not at serious enough exposure to be at risk, and in our discussions, she felt a lot more at ease knowing she was not in any peril to develop hand or wrist problems when demonstrating the vibrators to customers. Even the specter of capillary damage was minimal, much to her relief.

Many of our colleagues asked us if we were offered any free samples of the product lines for either souvenirs or for simply experimentation. You know, like extras, overruns, quality rejects, overstock, etc. Well, the truth of the matter is yes, we were offered some free samples by our customer service oriented young lady, and took about a half dozen or so.

But then we simply shipped them all back to Agatha (you remember her from the turkey story) because we knew her supply was limited and probably beginning to show the aging effects of high mileage.

Conclusion

As far as safety and Ergonomics is involved, it is always better to be prepared in any form of any potential injury event, no matter how absurd the job or how any adverse at-risk condition may effect worker health. Truly this was a case which had all the concerns of worker safety and health. We were pleased we could put them on the right track to establish a good safety & Ergonomics program eliminating at-risk conditions ensuring a proactive approach to worker health.

Incidentally, a photo of the product board does not grace our conference room wall for obvious reasons. However, it is hidden discretely in our scrapbook and is readily available whenever we need a portfolio review with a prospective client.

The Ergonomic UPS (uninterruptible power source)

PSS Eco 1400VA UPS

FEATURES: Ergonomic Design - Australian output plugs - Wide input voltage range - Boost and... more info

$249.00

PRICE

category: Power Surge Protection, Power, UPS & Surge Protection,

http://www.arrowcomputers.com.au/products-page/
uninterruptible-power-supplies-ups/

You all know what a UPS unit is, also known as a Battery Backup, or in the techie world an Uninterruptable Power Source. Hence it is called a UPS, not to be confused with the package / mail carrier. It protects against power outages and kicks in within nanoseconds to protect your precious data from being lost...a lifesaver in many cases.

However, when you buy one you only handle it once, plug in your computer, plug the UPS system into the wall and then shove the whole thing under your desk or workbench and forget it for a lifetime.

Of course, you will surmise, advertisements tout them as Ergonomic, it's in the ad and they can't lie in ads can they? Being curious, I called a manufacturer. I got the receptionist.

"Can you tell me why your UPS system, Model such-and-such is listed as Ergonomic?"

She said "You'll have to talk to sales. I'll transfer you."

"Thanks", I said. "Please do."

"Sales", a nice voice said.

"Yes, Can you tell me why your UPS system, Model such-and-such is listed as Ergonomic?"

She said "You'll have to talk to Engineering. I'll transfer you."

Thanks, Please do."

"Engineering", a matter-of-fact voice said.

"Yes, Can you tell me why your UPS system, Model such-and-such is listed as Ergonomic?"

Ergo Scene V - Ergonomic UPS

"Well, you'll have to talk to Design Styling. I'll transfer you."

Thanks", "Please do."

Next came another nice voice "Design Styling"

"Yes, Can you tell me why your UPS system, Model such-and-such is listed as Ergonomic?"

"Sure can", an upbeat voice answered.

"I'm really curious."

"Well...we researched this problem and it's Ergonomic because the pilot light is on the front so you can see if it is on or off."

I furrowed my brows "What?" I thought to myself.

I formulated a quick response. "Well what if the light was located on the back" I replied.

"Then you couldn't tell if it were on of off and it wouldn't be Ergonomic" came the reply.

I thought what an evasive answer.

So I said "If the UPS system was not on, your computer wouldn't be working and it would be a little obvious wouldn't it?"

She replied "*Yes, but we like to make it easy or Ergonomic for the operator to know if their computer is on or off.*

I said "Let me get this straight, you folks put the pilot light on the front to make it more Ergonomically correct (sic), isn't that kind of pushing what Ergonomics is all about? By the way, what kind of research did you do?"

I immediately got a dial tone.

clipart.com

Ergo Scene VI.

Young Love -A Real Success Story

On a recent project with a steel cable making company in the Midwest, the project involved heavy manual materials handling. The project involved coiling up steel cables from humongous ginormous big 10 foot reels into smaller "man" or human sized (to be politically correct) 4 foot coils for use in reinforced post tensioned concrete structures or cable structures like the Golden Gate Bridge in San Francisco.

Ergo Scene VI - Young Love

Once the smaller coils were wound up from the ginormous big coils, they were manually picked up and taken through the following sequence:

- carried over the shoulder a distance
- placed on the floor and end capped
- picked up, carried over the shoulder a ways
- dropped back on the floor
- press on an anchor with a big machine
- picked up, carried a ways over the shoulder
- dumped on the floor again
- spray painted for later color code identification
- picked back up, carried over the shoulder to a staging rack
- finally lifted up to hang onto the rack like a big coat hook.

Now, all that carryin', liftin', pushin', and shovin', requires a certain amount of muscle power. All the workers on this line were pretty buff with well muscled arms, and lean bodies. No pot bellies here with a daily workout like this with these smaller coils weighed in at 80 pounds to 200 pounds. In fact in observing this entire scenario, it resembled a real cardiovascular workout combined with an iron pumping regimen. No gym fees required. Meek and under nourished need not apply.

One of the young bucks I got to work with was the epitome of physical health. He's tall, about 6'-2", good looking, broad shoulders, and probably had a six-pack.

In short, a body like Adonis and it easily showed even through his company coveralls. He was a wide receiver until an injury cut his athletic career short. He also had a great smile and a wonderful personality. He and I worked well together

He showed me all the ins and outs of this particular job tasking, and encouraged me to perform the whole rotation from beginning to end, just so I could get a real "feel" for it.

After about three or four cycles, these old bones couldn't take it any more and I turned the job back over to him. By then I had a real appreciation of how hard the job really was. He told me I had great potential if I ever needed a job and that I just needed to get into a little better shape. I said 'thanks."

We worked together for awhile exchanging ideas on how to minimize the handling and potential injuries. In fact management to their credit understood these guys were "bustin' their chops" all day long pushin' and liftin' these heavy coils and this was indeed taking its toll.

Even my Adonis friend admitted he was hurtin' at the end of a shift when heavy coils were scheduled and run. Imagine what it was doing to an aging workforce.

After a few sessions with the entire work crew and management, a design was developed to address all excessive lifting and carrying.

A solution developed involving a methods change and an installation of some overhead tracks and electric quick lifting hoists…a most elegant solution. It worked well and the entire crew benefited. And according to them, it made the job so much easier by greatly reducing the lifting and carrying tasks. In fact, my Adonis friend admitted it wasn't the same workout it used to be.

In a follow-up session about a month later, I saw my Adonis friend. He waved me over and fist bumped me.

He said "I just wanted to tell you about the effects of your Ergonomic modifications."

"Oh yeah, good or bad?" I replied returning the fist bump.

"Both", he said.

"OK, give me the bad first. I can take it."

"Well, this job isn't as much of a workout as before."

"Isn't that the whole point", I replied.

"Yeah, but before you guys changed it, I really worked up a sweat. With your Ergonomics, it's not so much of a workout, and I'm slipping out of shape. So now, to keep in shape, I have to spend more time at the gym and it cuts into my personal time", he giggled.

"And on top of that, the gym raised my dues to full membership, since I'm there more often, so your project here cost me more money", he continued with a big smile.

"Oh, uhh sorry" was all I could think of to say.

"Well, so uhh, what's the good news" I said in a crafty ploy to change the subject.

He laughed and said. "The good news is that I feel much more energetic when I get home. I'm not so beat up and tired. And that's just on the plus side."

"There's more?" I inquired, waiting for the punch line.

"Man Yeah" he said enthusiastically. "My girlfriend wanted me to specifically tell you THANK YOU, because now that I'm more rested and energetic, I'm more active in our love life. And she REALLY likes that. She now thinks that Ergonomics is the greatest and she specifically told me to tell you that."

"You serious?" I said puzzled.

"Yeah."

And with that, he gave me a big slap on the shoulder, another hearty fist bump, AND WALKED AWAY SMILING AND CHUCKLING.

Ahhh Yes, L'amour!!

clker.com

Is Your Butt Ergonomic?

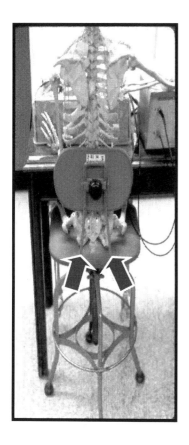

This is our lab skeleton, his name is Mr. Bones, as in "Working Them to the…"

He is exhibiting the two major bumps that you sit on located at the lower end of the pelvic girdle (arrows), named ischial tuberosities. These are the bony protuberances that push down through the gluteal muscles (gluteus maximus) – commonly known as your behind, butt or in some instances...the can, trying to push themselves though the muscle, fascia and skin. These are the high pressure points of your behind.

High pressure on these points causes pain and discomfort. This is the main reason you fidget in a chair or stand up simply to relieve this pain.

This is why hard chairs are so uncomfortable. This is the reason you love your "couch potato" couch. This is also the reason you don't like hard benches. Wheelchair bound folks have a real issue with this obviously because they can't feel the pain and the associated injury that goes along with it. Consider yourself fortunate if you can feel this discomfort.

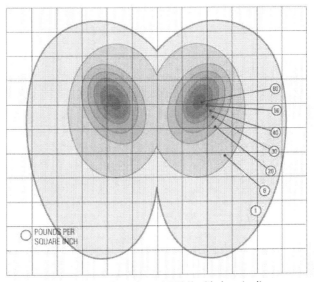

Pressures Developed While Sitting (psi)

Here is a pressure map of a butt placed on a flat surface. It was probably done with a fancy pressure plate in a fancy lab. The numbers are in PSI or pounds per square inch. You'll notice the highest pressures are right on your "sit bones."

If you were laying down flat on your back, face up under a glass bottom chair – and someone dropped their trousers and then sat down on said chair, this is what you would see.

I HAVE ABSOLUTELY NO IDEA WHY YOU WOULD EVER BE IN THAT POSITION, BUT IF INDEED YOU WERE, THIS IS WHAT YOU WOULD SEE.

You'll note that the point of highest pressure is exactly where the ischial tuberosities are, one on either side of the posterior cleavage, with the pressure incrementally reducing in concentric circles surrounding the ischial tuberosities.

Real Scientific Stuff.

Now, I once had a couple of students who wanted to really prove this concept in more than just big words and fancy engineering graphs.

How did they do it? I'm Glad you asked…

Go On…Take a Look!!!

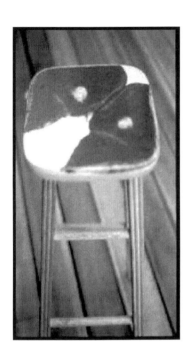

This is how they did it.

They went to the school lab, dropped their trousers, lathered themselves up with printers ink and sat down on this stool.

Now, I,…um, ..I,….I didn't actually see this experiment, but I imagine it was very…well...interesting to say the least.

You can see the two spots on the stool where the pressure exerted by the ischial tuberosities was so great that it literally squeezed the ink, forcing it out from under the gluteal muscles and now only the original paint shows through the (ahem) impression.

This is one reason it hurts to sit on a hard surface. This is how your butts communicate their displeasure. *Because like Mama, "If your Butt ain't happy, then ain't nobody happy."*

So you should really listen to your butt!

Proof positive that there is scientific basis for designing chairs and other things, like workstations around the human body (Ergonomics).

Of course in the design of anything around the human anatomy should be based on sound scientific principles and not just placing the word Ergonomic in front of it or in the product description (see appendix for absurdities of this manner).

Any relationship design to the human performance or resting should be well founded in proven scientific principles with lots and lots of forethought, as in design iterations.

Think about it and pay attention,

Your Butt is Smarter Than You Think!

Ergo Scene VIII
Unaware Underwear Ergonomics

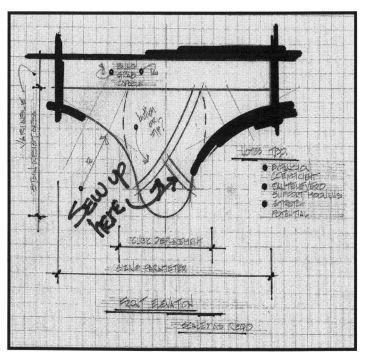

Lots of people don't really know how Ergonomics relates to someone actually doing something. Here we'll analyze, not a work task, but a task and piece of equipment almost every male contends with on a daily and very personal basis.

This is a task requiring utmost dexterity, delicate equipment handling and of course proper functioning (Ergonomic) design. In summation, it means this task should be safer, easier, and more efficient - and, by default, more convenient. It is a task touching (pardon the pun) many small Ergonomic details of regular life whether you know it or not.

Men's underwear is the subject. There are nuances of this particular piece of men's clothing that most folks, including men are not really aware of. This may or may not be a problem. Suffice it to say that functioning of these undergarments is oftentimes overlooked and design abounds with differing types, styles and functionality. A known fact is that no real collective solution exists for everyone, even though some Ergonomists espouse that a truly valid solution is a universal fit for all anatomical structures.

Often overlooked in Ergonomic design circles for some unknown reason, perhaps lack of data, is that not every male is the same size, structure, configuration or style. These variables definitely fall out of the typical small, medium or large denomination. Additionally it is quite obvious to everyone, that not all personages use the same handling technique for the various activities. Although size call outs are primarily for numerical waist size dimensions, sometimes simply stated in single, even multiple alphabet letters, there is no provisioning for the assembly of various other anatomical elements.

The overriding fallacy here is Ergonomic is often but mistakenly means one size (ahem) fits all. Go ahead and Google Ergonomic Underwear and you will find a bunch of, yes, absurd things. Are they really Ergonomic or not? Well there is and undoubtedly will always be an argument.

All clothes should, by nature be comfortable and mostly functional. Major exceptions being things like skin tight jeans, high heels and European slim cut suits, whose designers make them so closely form fitting that you have no choice but to know you have their suit on. The best Ergonomic feature is when you get to take them off.

First of all Ergonomics shouldn't be stated in the same realm of comfort, not like fancy, rugged, L.L. Bean flannel hunting shirts, that do a lot of things including being long lasting and manly looking. By default any piece of clothing in order to function well should be by default comfortable.

So what is all this about men's underwear? Aren't they just supposed to protect, comfort, coddle and support the man's manliness? Well in truth, other than a diapers function one doesn't not necessarily need to wear these under garments underneath a pair of dress or casual pants for functional reasons. Save for drips, smears and other leakage, which Pampers or adult diapers protect us from, the general men's underwear doesn't really seem to necessarily do anything. It sometimes just gets in the way when one is in a hurry, real hurry, if you get my drift.

In these days of baggy pants and shorts style, underwear has a newfound purpose. Even the new wave basketball players - pros on down to club teams, are showing modesty with layers and layers of undergarments. Unlike Wilt "the Stilt" Chamberlain who had nearly three feet of skin showing with short shorts and high socks, the current basketball trend is just the opposite, showing less skin. In this way underwear has a distinct purpose in the modesty area.

In exploring this modesty string, what would a proud Scotsman have to protect himself from curious little kids sneaking a peek up his kilt if it were not for underwear? Or how would he protect himself from wandering eyes when seated and he inadvertently crosses his legs in a typical "figure 4" manly style. There exists a comical well known photograph circulating the internet showing a complete frontal shot of The Queen properly dressed and seated amongst a troop of Scotsmen. The Scotsmen are all in full regalia, formally attired in Kilts and berets for what seems to be a typical group memorabilia photo shoot. All kilts are appropriately positioned effectively hiding everyone's "personals", excepting one, naturally, the one seated directly beside The Queen. Of course, everything is out in full view and there is usually a humorous quip to accompany said photo (key words: queen, kilts, exposure). It is undoubtedly Photoshopped in some manner; I'd really hate to think this is a real photo. However, it does illustrate exactly how men's undergarments function as a modesty panel.

In looking at pure function, typical men's underwear, often called briefs or shorts, try to address some specific things:

- Protection
- Coddling
- Insulation
- Drips

One outstanding item on this list is the protection aspect. Yes, men's' packaging surely does need a high level of protection from outward forces, like thrown objects, punches, kicks and the like. However protection of these precious items is always at the forefront of the subconscious mind. In the animal kingdom the family jewels are generally 'hanging out" so to speak, with no outwardly protection at all, no fancy loin cloths or modesty panels, save other than being tucked way underneath between a couple of muscular legs and (usually) a tail. Combined with a natural ferocity of fangs, claws and a couple hundred pounds of animal muscle, plus attitude, security is generally pretty high.

For civilized man standing in an upright bipedal position, these precious items are positioned right out in the open. Similar in scope to a sidewalk lamp fastened onto a wall. Not much surrounding it for protection, other than whatever guard or device is on the premises, especially for those going "Commando".

Therefore underwear may simply be an additional protective device in addition to trousers, placing layers of protection between the precious commodities and the outside world.

Protection INDEED! Surely, you have watched the television show Americas Funniest Videos. They delight at almost every episode to present various chapters of male occurrences aptly named "Groin Shots." With these, the audience either laughs heartedly or exclaims OOOO, not in sympathy, but in complete empathy with the subject in the aftermath of a punch, hit, kick or whatever in the sensitive areas. The scene is generally followed with a soulful moan, anguish cry and expression of extreme pain while the victim tries to sooth his excruciating discomfort while wallowing in the fetal position.

With the awareness of such known dangers and within the complexities of protection, there seems a school of thought to really encase these items in a vault so strong that only one possible means of access is available. But what about egress and ingress for certain periodic bodily functions? Hence the fly is invented both for the trousers and the underwear.

The trousers evolved a zipper for easy and convenient means for opening and closing. The underwear simply followed suit by developing a series of overlapping, highly articulated flaps to keep things protected minimizing risk of accidentally flopping out. To get the plumbing out for those certain moments these flaps must be negotiated, navigated, or moved aside.

Additional searching, pulling and tugging to align all appropriate equipment through the openings and through the zipper for appropriate action is also often required.

Herein lies an additional problem. All that pulling, tugging and negotiating to get the thing out, requires the same action is required for getting everything back in. A difficulty often faced is the specter of the flaps inadvertently and uncomfortably surrounding and chocking off said apparatus. With certain types and brands of underwear, it is often quite cumbersome, a fact known to all men.

Oftentimes the configuration of specialized underwear does not allow one to easily perform this tucking in chore efficiently. With this cumbersome tucking in problem and especially with one being in a hurry or having man size apparatus, what happens? The package is not neatly and appropriately tucked in and is left half hanging out. In hurry up mode, the owner in trying to unsuccessfully get everything back under the layers often misjudges the timing, frantically pulling the zipper up in a forceful and quick manner before everything else is positioned correctly.

What happens next is pain beyond belief when ones' little Willie is caught inadvertently in the teeth of a Levi's style heavy duty metal zipper. The owner immediately screams, does three quick laps around the shop, doing his utmost in frantically trying not to make a scene and finally settles down in a chair with hands between legs, knees together trying to soothe and protect himself. Try and look nonchalant and inconspicuous here.

Therefore what was attempted at a protective mode actually is contributory to an event of horrific pain, embarrassment and significant lost time in repair and recuperation.   Know this, Band Aids do not generally fit this particular anatomical appendage due to frequent skin tension and shape changes.

So the protection mode, from a design stand point does not generally cover all bases and obviously an issue of concern for all males and the design team.

For the remainder of the list or if none are required, what good is underwear? Maybe all men would be better off not using any at all. I have observed that many of the younger and hip crowd, even young girls wear the underwear on the outside of trousers, being a fashion choice. And to think how wrong I was to think that underwear should be worn on the inside. Ho!

But, for the main functioning of briefs as an entity in themselves are they really needed? Well let's just say for the sake of discussion, that they are, being worn 90% of the time for whatever reason. Maybe it's the same as parading around in a fashionable pair of gym or running shorts. So what is the difference?

Briefs tend to be, well just that brief, and some of the new styles have stretch fabric characteristics, meaning they hug the hip, upper leg and personal items in a sleek fashion to help the manly man look a little sleeker and perhaps sexier, when he doesn't have anything else on.

Here's where the Ergonomics or lack of Ergonomics come into play.

Given that many men like the sleek cool, form-fitting style because it makes them feel more hip and more "moderne", this style works no better than the baggy boxer types. It doesn't really matter much here because the problem is universally the same. The point may be an isolated one, but I do know that the following perception exists and probably to the chagrin of those designing, making and wearing men's underwear.

Men must relieve themselves, sometimes often, occurring when watching a ball game where a lot of fluids like beer are consumed, on hot days at backyard barbeques, or anywhere food and drink are part and parcel of the activities. Often times, the situation is such that the relief event becomes an emergency situation, requiring a tight control of the lower abdominal or deep pelvic musculature simply to keep the outlet valve closed, and closed tight. Sometimes it may not be a social emergency, but merely a shortage of facilities, a long line or maybe a significant distance to the nearest loo. Whatever the case, without proper muscle tone, a visible uncontrolled leakage catastrophe could occur with potentially socially awkward or disastrous occurrences.

This brings us to that other wonderful and unique Ergonomic invention in men's clothing, "the fly," a simple opening in the undergarment to allow the man to let out his manliness and aim it appropriately, even in hurry-up emergency situations.

Note that the fly relating to men's pants or underwear is spelled the same as the insect variety. I proffer the following for those interested on how this personal opening came to be named after a common household pest. Well, it really isn't. The term fly refers to a piece of cloth that covers an opening or object or shields something from something else.

Those familiar with tents know, a rain fly is simply a big piece of cloth acting as a rain shield either for the tent or for an opening. There, now you know.

Ever seen a rain fly?
♫
How about a horse fly ?
Seen a dragon fly?
Maybe a shoe fly?
Surely you've seen a house fly?
♫
Disney characters will tell you about
Seeing a peanut stand
Listening to a rubber band
They even claim to have seen a
Polka dot railroad tie
♫
They mostly claim to have seen just about everythin'
When they see an _____ fly
♫

Talking about flys, or flies, here is the best subject matter joke I know:

*What **three magic words** can a girl fly say to a boy fly to make him immediately blush?*

Your human's open.

Okay, here we go with the real Ergonomics stuff.

Way back in college, I remember a creative social event. Like today, sororities and fraternities often have creative one-upmanship pranks or some such activities. It began with a local sorority having it in for a rival or "associated fraternity", whatever that means. Plans were made to "get the boys."

With clandestine observation, planning and such, the sorority sisters found out when the frat house would be empty. A black ops sorority squad was sent in to pilfer the boys' undergarments and return to the sorority house, whereupon a bevy of seamstress activity took place in hurriedly sewing all the flies shut on said boys undergarments. Naturally this had to be done quickly, enabling the black ops squad to get all the underwear back into the boys' dressers and rooms without being discovered. I wondered if they even collected those in the dirty laundry hampers.

The girls thought they had triumphed over the boys big time. They waited and waited and waited for some signal that their prank had really inconvenienced the boys.

Actually several weeks, perhaps months passed before the boys even started noticing. It appears the girls had greatly misunderstood the Ergonomics of using men's, underwear, both briefs and boxer styles.

In revealing interviews, the girls assumed the boys needed the fly to do their business in relieving themselves after one of their weekly frat keggers. Not so. The reporter covering this story interviewed both the fraternity brothers and sorority sisters, at least those who would volunteer to go on record (anonymous of course) and found out that the brothers rarely used the fly for anything. Subsequent queries to typical male students on campus had similar results. That is that boys rarely use the fly part of underwear, and when Mother Nature calls, they simply pull the whole thing to the side and use the larger leg opening. This functions well even if the underwear is worn backwards, which can conceivably occur during a hangover after a kegger, early in the morning in bad light with blurry vision and being late for class. In this case the fly is unavailable anyway.

Looking closer at the big picture, there does not even seem to be a need for a fly. Maybe that is why the bikini type of underwear remains popular. Even some of today's fashions dictate other extreme methods. For instance, when there is purposely no fly available, what do you do? In the case of sweat pants which are generally loose fitting and worn over running shorts, jock straps and other under-the-pants type of gear, a simple one hand action is all that's needed. One simply grabs a handful of the sweat pants at the elastic waist band along with a secure cluster of the other paraphernalia and simply pulls all the bunched up clothing below critical level for proper draining activities.

The sisters figured by sewing up all the flies, the wearer would be placed in a compromised emergency mode or social context, much to the wearers' dismay.

The boys surely couldn't pull this sweat pants "all quickly down to critical level" move because in my day pants were slimmer about the waist. Sweat pants and such were not de rigueur dress and most everyone wore a belt making a hurried full pull down even more difficult. If all went as planned, this should have resulted in an obvious source of humor and story telling for the sisters. Truly a tale destined to live in infamy, forever treasured in the annals of sorority lore. Unfortunately, it turned out the brothers hardly noticed that the sorority gals had even done anything to their precious underwear.

The overall conclusion here is that the sisters had a really bad misunderstanding of functionality and task performance of the manly package and how it is used in ordinary and emergency situations (Underwear Ergonomics). They didn't perform an appropriate Ergo analysis. If they had, their approach would obviously have been different.

In reality, by nature of underwear design to fit the male pelvic area, often fabricated to show off specific men's' attributes, it also contributes to the overall problem itself. Moving through layers and layers of clothing to get something done goes directly against the grain of good design. Here form should indeed follow function.

Here is an example, almost everyone can relate to in some form or another. Ever had to scratch an incurable incessant itch buried under layers and layers of insulating clothing while tobogganing in sub zero weather? You know very well that to get to that itch you must first mess around with layers upon layers of clothing that was donned with great care, in specific order when in the comfort of the lodge. Each piece was carefully tightened and sealed up to protect against the cold. Unfastening the seals and layers was only to be done after the tobogganing was completed.

Unfastening these garments is difficult to begin with and under emergency situations made more difficult with big gloves on and the exposure of raw flesh to Mother Natures onslaught. A heavy tariff simply for sensory relief. If the itch (or other bodily occurrences) is that irritating or offending and you simply can't stand it, then the penalty might just be worth it. Trying to do something the garments we wear were not designed for, oftentimes leads to less than stellar results and possibly injury (metal zipper?). Ask yourself this question: How would you design around this problem? Remember the bottom flap in full cover pajamas little kids used to wear? Maybe there is some design inspiration from that.

Obviously the fly can become simply too cumbersome to navigate even under the most friendly circumstances, whether you have help or not. A full critiques shows the fly is indeed in need of a revisit, to ascertain exactly what the requirements are for modern mans' needs for emergency egress, emergency ingress, friendly persuasion and overall safety.

These things are at the very heart of Ergonomic design and should be revisited to help the modern male.

Homework

So, for you guys, the next time you go to the men's room, do a quick Ergo analysis, and see how you handle yourself when trying to get yourself clear of your undergarments and see if you do indeed negate the fly in totality or actually use this designed-in opening effectively and efficiently.

I'll wager that there are multitudes of differing methods, techniques and probably some very unique and creative ways to get this done. The differing methods will no doubt be accompanied by various opinions on what is the most efficient and seamless means. Does Jockey underwear have a better fly design than Fruit-of-the-Loom? Or how much faster are you at the draw if you don't use underwear at all and are you saving precious man-seconds in getting back to that critical meeting or to those front row seats at the playoff game?

The frat boys went on record, saying using the fly is too cumbersome. It just takes too long to locate and navigate through and to get your package out to the appropriate position. Especially in time sensitive situations, those precious few seconds can make the difference between real embarrassment, fumbling your piece or simply being able to continue gracefully through your social event.

Surprisingly, no mention was given about left or right hand handling or for the associated directional orientation of the fly. An obvious question put forth by a learned Ergonomist would be: Should the fly be oriented to the left allowing a right handed approach to the initial pull aside action? Or is an opening properly oriented to the right side allowing a left hand approach leaving the usually dominant right hand free for other delicate functions. Which dominant hand should take precedence?

I'm sure there are arguments for this left side or right side opening orientation however, is there really a sense of efficiency and correctness related to the way the openings are designed? I wonder if anyone loses sleep at night pondering what could be critical design decisions to a garment universally used by a large segment of the population.

Hence the task performance of using the fly obviously still needs of some careful analysis in terms of Ergonomics before final decisions can be made. What is optimum configuration? Or in fact are undies needed at all? The answer for these questions may give the term Ergonomic Underwear some real meaning after all.

In Conclusion to the Absurd

Remember these were real jobs performed by real people and we had to respect that. We had to be unbiased in the job type, job subject and do our best to take care of potential and current injuries as best we could. This is regardless of what all other folks thought of our interaction with all these workers.

After all that is our job yours and mine being Ergos. We have to somehow provide creative solutions, keep workers working, getting them out of pain, helping them support their families. Absurd as some of these jobs are, that's really the bottom line.

This is truly what good Ergonomists should do and what good Ergonomics is about, even if in fields which seem well, a little absurd.

Of course there are elements of being *REALLY ABSURD* - check out the following worker compensation story line from (reportedly) Reuters.

News flash from Reuters

Phone Sex Worker Injured in Line of Duty

November 19 1999 at 09:51pm

Miami - A Florida phone sex operator has won a workers' compensation settlement claiming she was injured after regularly masturbating at work, her lawyer said.
Attorney Steven Slootsky said he was not sure whether the Fort Lauderdale woman's claim was the first of its kind, but it certainly was out of the ordinary.

Slootsky said his client agreed to a "minimal settlement" earlier this month. He declined to disclose the amount. During the course of her claim for workers' compensation benefits, the now 40-year-old employee of Fort Lauderdale's CFP Enterprises Inc, *said she developed carpal tunnel syndrome - also known as repetitive motion injury* - in both hands from masturbating as many as seven times a day while speaking with callers, said Slootsky, who spoke about the case this week on the condition that his client's name not be revealed.

"She was told to do whatever it takes to keep the person on the phone as long as possible," Slootsky said.
The woman used one hand to answer the telephone and the other to note customers' names and fetishes and to give herself an orgasm during the verbal exchanges.

The calls usually lasted about 15 minutes, although callers who asked for the woman by name were given 30 minutes of talk time, Slootsky said. In her petition for workers' compensation benefits, filed with Florida's Department of Labor and Employment Security in April, the woman claimed she received her injury from "repetitive use of the phone."

She claimed weekly benefits of $267 a week - based on an annual weekly wage of $400 - and also asked to be reimbursed for $30,000 in medical bills after a neurosurgeon operated on her hands to relieve her pain.

Slootsky said his client was too embarrassed to tell her doctor the real cause of her injury and the lack of disclosure led a mediator to advise her that she would have difficult case to prove at trial. - Reuters

Source : http://www.iol.co.za/news/back-page/phone-sex-worker-injured-in-line-of-duty-1.20189

A Collection of

Things Labeled

Ergonomic

Which Really Aren't

(it's just a marketing ploy)

Please don't be duped by

The Hype

Why are all those things called Ergonomic?

Right now, Ergonomics is becoming a known and accepted concept. However, there are those who would use the term in the most absurd way, simply to market their product, whether Ergonomic or not. the word Ergonomic or Ergonomically designed is being used as a facetious marketing term which falsely means their product is better. Nothing could be further from the truth.

If it says it's Ergonomic on the label or on the box, it probably isn't!!!!

The marketplace if filled with false and sometimes useless Ergonomic things like:

* Ergonomic Potato Chips
* Ergonomic Dog Toys
* Ergonomic Nose Hair Clipper
* Ergonomic Toilet Seat
* Ergonomic Jock Straps

    and Ergonomic _____ (fill in the blank)

Well GUESS WHAT? Some if not all of these things are not really Ergonomic in the sense of helping someone reduce potential injury, being easier to use or improving any type of task performance (especially the toilet seat). Ergonomics here is used solely as a marketing term - so BUYER BEWARE!!!!! Do not be misled by misinformation.

A Collection of Things Ergonomic...*NOT*

Take a Look !!!!
As we uncover more absurd Ergonomic things, we will be updating this publication periodically.

Share with us the results of shopping in stores, our various purchases and research on the internet. Did some "Ergonomic" thought go into these. Maybe...maybe not. Emphasis is on the not!

Maybe it's made of high friction material to keep you from sliding off
http://www.akw-ltd.co.uk/?s=ergonomic+toilet+seat&cat=3

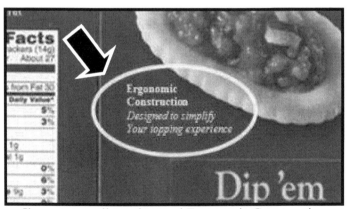

I've never really understood Ergonomic Construction
(Author's Collection)

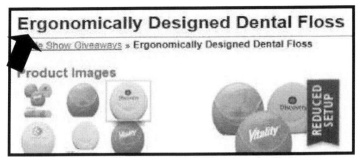

Do you floss your teeth Ergonomically?
(http://www.qualitylogoproducts.com/tradeshow-promotions/ergonomically-designed-dental-floss.htm)

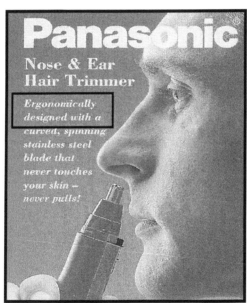

Helps keep your nose hairs Ergonomic
(Author's Collection)

Even cats need Ergonomics - NOT
(www.whiskerstudio.com)

I'm not sure if pillows contouring Ergonomically to the pet
qualifies as an Ergonomic item
(http://exoticdogs.com/default.asp?lvlA=22&lvlB=154)

More Ergonomic items for dogs, of course
(http://www.etsy.com/listing/98776603/5-quart-20-inch-double-ergonomically)

For you City Slickers, a girth is the strap under the horse holding the saddle on!
(http://www.horse.com/item/tekna-ergonomic-all-purpose-girth/E000445)

An Ergonomic hook is what every earring should have
(http://www.catherinecardellinipearls.com/?subject=earrings)

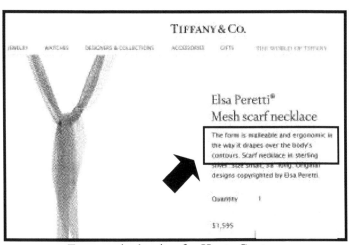

Ergonomic draping for Haute Couture
(http://www.tiffany.com/Shopping/Item.aspx?sku=10659515)

Ergonomical? like comical...

What?

www.packatraxxx.com

Not really a bad idea

(http://www.thewritingpenstore.com/p-122-crayon-rocks-ergonomic-crayons-treasure-bag-of-16-summer-colors.aspx)

'Nuff said

(http://www.intomobile.com/2007/09/27/au-infobars-the-ergonomically-sexy-candybar-phone)

Another oxymoron

(http://www.zdnet.com/15-best-things-to-eat-as-you-tweet_p3-7000002475)

A flat floor means ergonomic?
(http://www.acousticalsurfaces.com/ergo_floor/ergo_floor.htm?d=16)

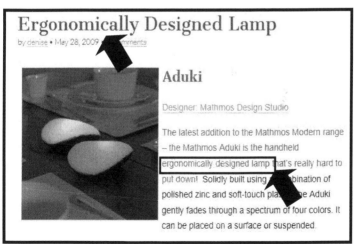

I didn't think lamps could be Ergonomic
(http://www.adistinctiveworld.net/ergonomically-designed-lamp)

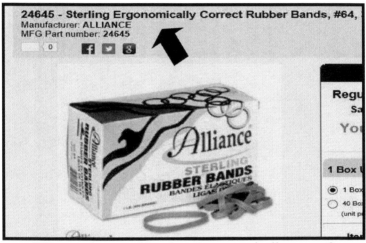

What makes a rubber band ergonomically correct?
(http://www.walmart.com/ip/14926534?wmlspartner=wlpa&adid=222222222270101300
61&wl0=&wl1=g&wl2=c&wl3=18140279950&wl4=&wl5=pla&wl6=40002407110&ve
h=sem#ProductDetail)

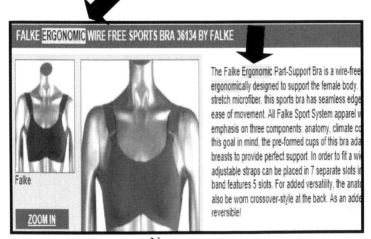

No comment
http://www.townshop.com/falke-ergonomic-wire-free-sports-bra_36134_s_p444.aspx

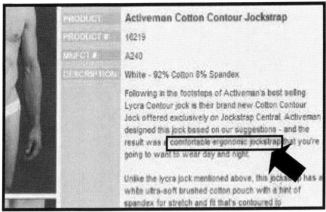

No comment

http://www.jockstrapcentral.com/productdisplay.php?product=16218

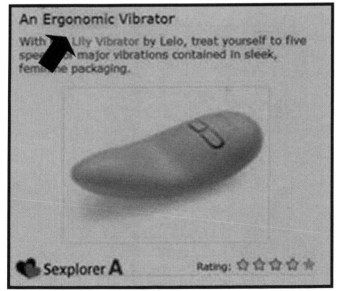

No Comment

http://www.redbookmag.com/love-sex/positions-toys-techniques/slrt-lily-vibrator

Ergonomics for the dog or owner?
(Author's Collection)

A Truely Ergonomic Invention

**We just couldn't resist including this bit of
imagination, showing off some fun we have with
Absurd Ergonomics**

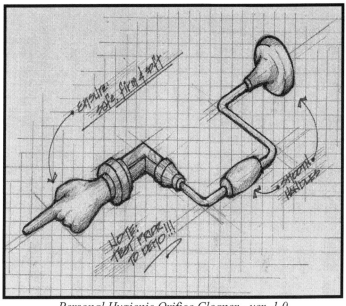

Personal Hygienic Orifice Cleaner - ver. 1.0

Throughout my career, I have been associated with
numerous inventors, tinkerers and mad scientists,
designing, building and trying to prove various tools,
and solutions for Ergonomic applications. Some are
practical, some turn out to be whimsical and some turn
out to be outright absurd - and some are just plain
useless.

Here is one of our late, late night ideas, the likes of which sneak into creative minds, attempting to solve what many would think is a serious social problem.

This shows you how extreme thinking can approach the development of real applications. It's not copyrighted or patented, nor do we make claim to any intellectual property. If this invention should make its way into some retail outlet and earns you a small fortune, all the best. Let us know and for providing the idea, we would appreciate a good steak dinner..

Background

This beloved inspiration is a design to make a daily personal and intimate chore more Ergonomic, safe and efficient. The overall approach was analyzing a task known for being socially unacceptable, especially in public places and generally performed in the privacy of one's own home. In reality, a necessary part of life generally performed several times per day.

The overriding feature is to mimic the actual task in such a way that this tool's function cannot be distinguished from using the real thing. In fact, it should be better than the real thing by virtue of its high mechanical advantage.

It's obvious that healthcare devices are popular "Holy Grails" to make oneself more beautiful, cleaner and healthier, by being more effective and efficient. Thus, this device is a natural for any beauty supply house, drugstore or Sharper Image type outlet.

Application

The user friendly Ergonomics allow even those who are "tool challenged" to use it with maximum success. It can be used to clean any human orifice, Maybe even ears or belly buttons. The imagination will also undoubtedly determine other appropriate placement. Special features include a very soft anatomically correct index finger for maximum comfort and cleaning, just like the real thing. It is designed to accept any brand latex glove to be later discarded for proper hygiene.

In actuality, this is an old school cordless drill known as a brace and bit. Highly portable and used where electrical power was non-existent or inconvenient, this tool is now generally found in tool museums, yard sales, dusty tool shops or in Grandpa's old wooden tool box hiding in the barn.

Fortunately, this means the handle part or brace can be economically available with the creative part only being in the business end. Thus prototyping is very budget friendly.

For true Ergonomic application to this device, simply make sure the grips are smooth without splinters and the business end is designed with utmost care. Who knows, with proper design and *chutzpah* you could earn a spot on TV's *Shark Tank*.

Even More

In these days of multi-use, given the Swiss Army
approach for tool versatility, a different end piece can
be interchanged specifically for performing another
one of man's most controversial of topics, one of the
high profile hot-button issues of our time. Not to
mention it being a heretofore un-Ergonomic task.

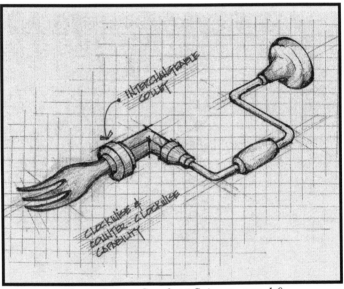

Haute Cuisine Spaghetti Spinner - ver. 1.0

Surely everyone has had trouble winding up spaghetti
at one time or another. History abounds with
documentation of vast efforts to solving this great
societal problem. The movie *Gizmo* (1977), full of old
news reels from the 20's about hilarious failed
inventions, depicts an inventor using a powered
spinning fork attempting to wind up spaghetti.

Astonishingly without any speed control the inventor remains deadly serious with his out of control spinner continually splattering spaghetti all over the room and himself.

Truly a madcap adventure. His oversight was simply lack of rotational (Ergonomic) control, unlike our highly featured and improved Ergonomic tool illustrated here.

Our versatile tool will undoubtedly make winding much easier and more Ergonomically efficient. When found in five star high-end restaurants, it will undoubtedly make great strides in improving the fine dining experience.

The Ergonomic intent was not necessarily to make either task one-handed, but to encourage the use of both hands affording maximum accuracy of placement, rotational control and proper delicate handling for said tasks. Warning! Continued use of only a single hand with these tools may predispose the user to a dreaded Repetitive Motion Injury by means of at-risk and awkward hand postures.

Double Warning! –real-time slow motion proof-of-concept testing is also highly recommended before going public with your invention.

A Definition of Ergonomics

Ergonomics is a very complex science, so much so that it currently defies a real definitive definition (how's that???) understandable and applicable to the everyday Joe. Depending on whom you talk to in the street you will get a different answer from the query "What do you think Ergonomics is?"

As many people think it is different things they all have kind of an ethereal understanding of its applications and nuances, however few ever get it right.

For your reading and educational pleasure, I proffer several definitions. All have merit and the most complete I feel is the one crafted by the International Ergonomics Society.

͵ər-gə-'nä-'mik-s - *adj*

As I've said, the definitions vary according to one's own knowledge of understanding and interpretation. To wit, even many of the dictionaries abound with differing definitions. Go ahead ask anyone what Ergonomics is…and you'll get: " it's a uhhh…umm…ahhh…well it's……" I guess dictionaries have the same problem.

A Definition of Ergonomics - con't

So, here's one simple definition.

*Safer, more productive work tasks
and workstations*

Complete, succinct and the average worker can relate
to and understand it, also immediately relating what it
can do for them. Company execs also find this
immediately understandable.

All right, all right, for those who would like a more
distinct definition, how's this, from pagaday.com,
workman publishing:

ûŕ-gho-nom-ik-x - *adj*: *designed or arranged for
safe, comfortable, and efficient use. - the science of
designing and arranging things people use so that the
people and things interact most efficiently and safely.*
(author's note; the definition should say ***efficient
human use***, with this definition being mangled, to wit
see the ergonomic dog toys in another chapter).

It is kind of a banal definition, it really leaves me kind
of flat. Totally uninteresting and stated in a manner
that really doesn't show potential, application or how
really beneficial the science can be.

A Definition of Ergonomics - con't

Here is another, from Wikipedia no less

Human factors and ergonomics (HF&E), *also known as comfort design, functional design, and user-friendly systems, is the practice of designing products, systems or processes to take proper account of the interaction between them and the people that use them.*

Not a word about safety and/or occupational injury.

Still a little incomplete and unsatisfying?

Here is probably one of, if not THE best, directly from the

IEA (International Ergonomics Association).
www.iea.cc

The IEA is essentially a group of 42 federated societies from around the world, and is a wonderful support group for any and all things Ergonomic.

If you are some kind of aspiring Ergo, Please, Please support them and at least visit their web page for more details. They really are doing wonderful things for the profession.

A Definition of Ergonomics - con't

Here's the IEA agreed definition of Ergonomics (2000)

Ergonomics helps harmonizing things that interact with people in terms of people's needs, abilities and limitations.

Derived from the Greek ergon (work) and nomos (laws) to denote the science of work, ergonomics is a systems-oriented discipline which now extends across all aspects of human activity. Practicing ergonomists must have a broad understanding of the full scope of the discipline. That is, ergonomics promotes a holistic approach in which considerations of physical, cognitive, social, organizational, environmental and other relevant factors are taken into account. Ergonomists often work in particular economic sectors or application domains. Application domains are not mutually exclusive and they evolve constantly; new ones are created and old ones take on new perspectives.

There exist domains of specialization within the discipline, which represent deeper competencies in specific human attributes or characteristics of human interaction.

Domains of specialization within the discipline of ergonomics are broadly the following;

- *Physical Ergonomics*
- *Cognitive Ergonomics*
- *Organizational Ergonomics*

Visit the IEA website for more detailed info on these domains of specialization. And support the organizations good work whenever and however you can!

A Definition of Ergonomics - con't

Author's note about definitions:

It seems that the science of Ergonomics is quickly expanding to include the many aspects of human life and tasks. Therefore a single complete definition may not be easily forthcoming.

The IEA definition, although lengthy, is this way simply to include the many various elements that the overall term Ergonomics encompasses. It may also be that the (your) definition might also just be limited to the specific application or project you are working on or involved with.

Such as;

- Computer Ergonomics
- Tool Ergonomics
- Chair Ergonomics
- Psychosocial Ergonomics
- Or Any Other Kind of Ergonomics

Naturally these valued definitions include many areas of Ergonomics of which the casual reader / user may not be aware of and naturally these aspects are well beyond the scope of this book.

A Definition of Ergonomics - con't

However, their inclusion may inspire some to perhaps follow their path and help advance the science.

And maybe when the term Ergonomics is bantered about in fancy dinner parties, the first question phrased should be the same when discussing engineering:

"And exactly what kind of ergonomics are we talking about?"

This would really help the definition center itself in good conversation and be clearer in the minds of those using the word, who also have vested interest in it.

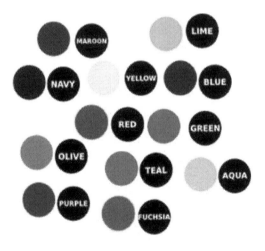

THANK YOU !!!

Thanks for being part of our Ergonomics world. I hope you have at least laughed, were entertained or were inspired and made some discoveries of your own.

If so, I would really love to hear about it (absurd or not). Maybe you would like feedback on one of your projects or just want to gab about Ergonomics .
We would also love hearing your feedback on our adventures.

Give us a poke if you would like knowing more about Real Ergonomists and their work!!

Alex
alex@ergonomicsoftheabsurd.com

Meanwhile, practice some Serious Ergonomics and make a positive impact on someone's life. They will thank you for it and you will be a much better person for it.

Remember Positive Karma.

You too can make a big change in someone's life!!!

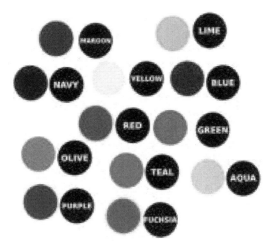

Acknowledgements

I gratefully acknowledge the following folks who have provided insight, critique, friendship, inspiration and company in my pursuit of completing this Ergonomic Adventure. Without whose help and friendship, I truly would not have been able to hit the finish line. My sincerest thanks goes to them and my apologies to those I have inadvertently left out. However, you know who you are and undoubtedly will never cease to give me grief to remind me of that.

I raise a glass to these folks for one reason or another, listed in no particular order.   Lance P., Paul S., Gary O., Sally C., Hannah S., Julie L., Matt M., Karl M., Lexi C. Jillian C., Paul A., Bill B. Jim B. , Susan L., Bill B., Sue T., Gordonzo, Sue R., AAAAron R., Jeff R., Jeffie J., Joanne B., Scott W., Craig W., Sue H., Joy S., Wayne M., Brian D., Sabrina S., Steve M., Ojo., Miriam J.

And of course to those staunch supporters in my Writing Club.: Doug M. Michele C, Kathy McM., Linda A., Ted Y., Chris G.

This Really Looks Cool in Full Color

Finis